Paintings by ORI SHERMAN

THE STORY OF HANUKKAH

told by AMY EHRLICH

DIAL BOOKS ⋈ NEW YORK

Published by Dial Books
A Division of Penguin Books USA Inc.
2 Park Avenue • New York, New York 10016
Published simultaneously in Canada by Fitzhenry & Whiteside Limited, Toronto
Text copyright © 1989 by Amy Ehrlich
Paintings copyright © 1989 by Ori Sherman
All rights reserved
Printed in the U.S.A.
Design by Atha Tehon
First Edition
E
1 3 5 7 9 10 8 6 4 2

Library of Congress Cataloging in Publication Data
Ehrlich, Amy, 1942–   The story of Hanukkah.
Summary: Retells the biblical story that is celebrated in the feast of Hanukkah.
1. Hanukkah—Juvenile literature. [1. Hanukkah.]
I. Sherman, Ori, ill. II. Title.
BM695.H3E4 1989   296.4'35   88-31109
ISBN 0-8037-0718-5
ISBN 0-8037-0719-3 (lib. bdg.)

Pictured on the frontispiece is a dreidel, a four-sided spinning top. On each side
is a Hebrew letter: nun (N), gimmel (G), heh (H), shin (SH). They stand for the Hebrew
words *Nes, Gadol, Hayah, Sham,* which mean "A Great Miracle Happened There."
On the nights of Hanukkah children play with the top, winning small prizes
such as nuts, raisins, or pennies.

The art for this book was created using gouache, a painting technique in
which opaque colors are ground in water and mixed with a preparation of gum.
Each painting was then color-separated and reproduced in full color.

DATE		
11/11	R0077004813	

In those days a king named Alexander reigned over the Jews, and he was merciful. But it happened that another who was called Antiochus came into the land. With a multitude of soldiers he came to Jerusalem and decreed that the Jews must forsake their laws. No longer could they keep the Sabbath or worship God in their temple. Now the Jews must bow down before idols and if any refused, they would die.

Long ago in the ancient land of Judea, the Jews dwelt in peace. They wanted only to worship God, to keep His laws, and to celebrate His glory.

Their temple in the holy city of Jerusalem stood on Mount Moriah for all to see. Within its walls were many precious objects, but among them was a simple lamp. For hundreds of years the Jews had kept it burning. Its strong, clear light showed the power of their faith.

For my grandnieces, Rachael and Heather

O. S.

————————————

For Aunt Ida and Cousin Johnny

A. E.

————————————

While faithful Jews watched in horror, the soldiers entered the temple itself. They placed an idol upon the golden altar and allowed pigs to run there. They drank from the holy vessels, and then they set fire to the books of the law.

The oil in the lamp was spilled and the light in the temple went out.

Now, in the town of Modin there dwelt a man called Mattathias, who had five sons. And when they saw what had been done to the temple of Jerusalem, they wept and mourned sorely. Never, they vowed, would they forsake God's laws.

The king's soldiers came and set an idol in the town, but Mattathias threw it down and called to the people, saying, "Whoever is for the Lord, come." Then he and his sons fled into the mountains, and many who sought justice also followed.

When the king was told that the Jews had gone down into the wilderness, he assembled a vast army. It was the Sabbath and the Jews were forbidden to fight.

But soldiers rose up in battle against them, slaughtering thousands. Then the Jews saw that they must fight even on the Sabbath.

At last Mattathias died and his son Judah the Maccabee led the Jews, for he was a great warrior. But the people were frightened and came to Judah, saying, "How can we who are so few fight against a multitude?"

That night under the starry sky Judah prayed to God, and when morning came he said to the people, "Do not be afraid, for the Lord is with us. Strength comes from heaven, it is not in the size of an army."

Then valiantly the Jews fought, defeating all the armies and generals that Antiochus could send against them. But when they marched triumphantly into Jerusalem and saw the temple abandoned and desolate, the strong soldiers began to weep.

Then Judah and those who were with him went up to cleanse the temple. They built the altar again according to the law and made new holy vessels and other precious things. At last it was time to light the lamp and rededicate the temple to God.

They searched all the rooms and courtyards until they found one cruse of pure oil the invaders had overlooked. But it was enough for only a day.

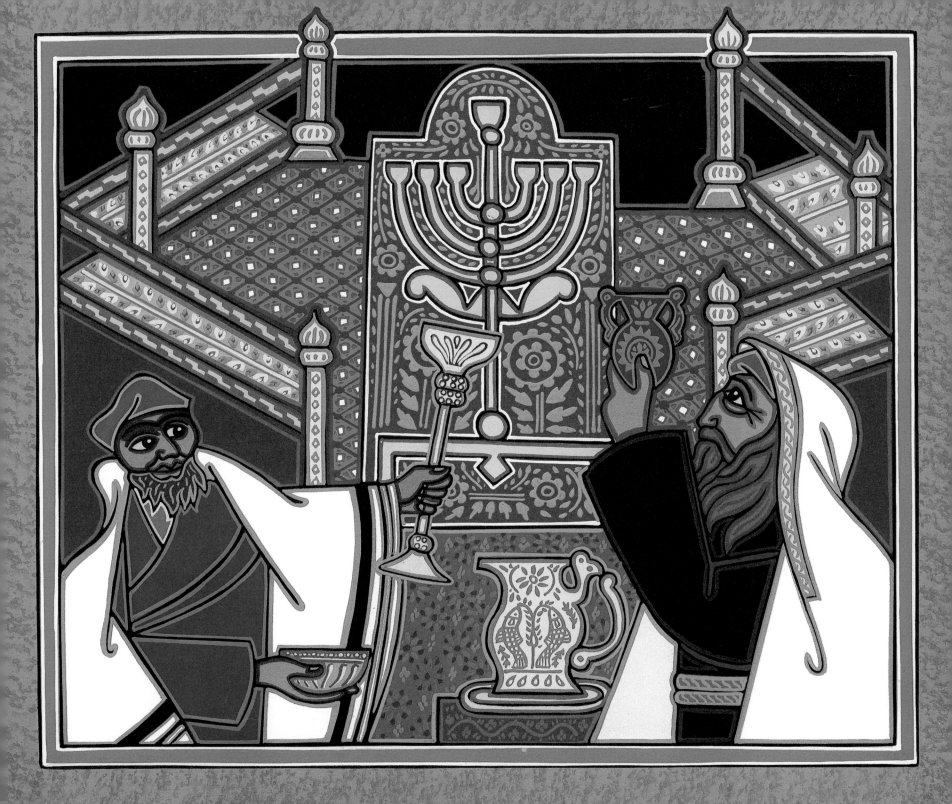

And after Judah saw this he took the cruse of oil in his hand and said to the people, "Let us yet rejoice in what we have and light the lamp to worship and praise God who has delivered us."

Then the people fell upon their knees and prayed.

They thought it would burn for only a day, but the oil in the lamp kept burning. Some said the flame grew brighter and brighter, illuminating every corner of the temple and dazzling the worshippers at their prayers.

And when more pure oil was finally made, the oil had burned for eight days and eight nights.

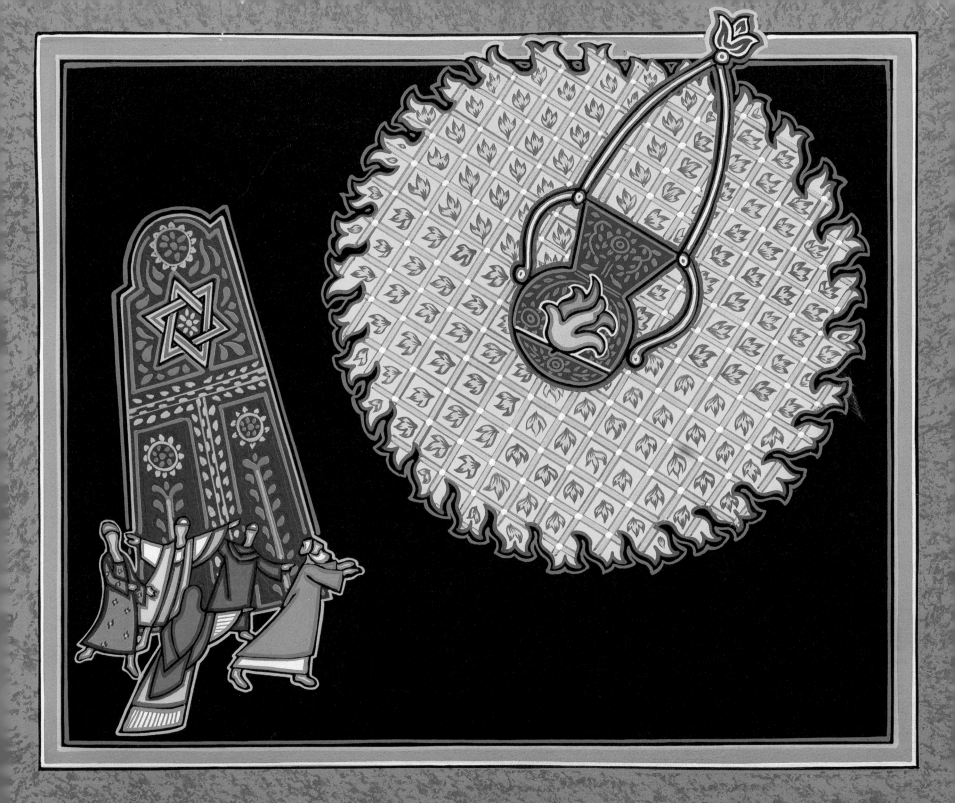

These events were in the Hebrew month of Kislev, beginning on the twenty-fifth day. Afterward Judah and his brothers decreed that the eight days of the rededication of the temple should be kept always in their season from year to year.

And so, like the oil of long ago, the lights of Hanukkah still burn brightly, proclaiming God's glory and the freedom of the Jews.